OPERATION
SPACE
QUEST
EPISODE THREE
MOON BASE

ISBN 978-1-59826-904-8

FELDHEIM PUBLISHERS
POB 43163, Jerusalem, Israel

Printed in Israel

OPERATION SPACE QUEST

EPISODE THREE
MOON BASE

A 3D GRAPHIC NOVEL BY

CHAIM VALDMAN

FELDHEIM PUBLISHERS

The hero of this book is Yossele Gewirtz, who, despite his desire to lead an ordinary life, is swept up in a drama so fascinating and so exciting that you, too, will undoubtedly be swept up the moment you begin reading.

History proves that there is a strong connection between the Jewish People and world events. More than once, a single Jew was the focus of a huge battle between powerful nations. In this story, it is up to young Yossele to rescue millions of people from an Islamic terrorist. The plot of this story is, of course, fictitious, but the concepts expressed in it, as well as various technical descriptions — are all based on fact.

The five bestselling Hebrew editions culminating the entire saga of Yossele's adventures have taken the Israeli Chareidi publishing world by storm, opening up a new genre and standard in religious 3-D comics. The English editions will start with Episode 3, the most relevant story to today's world events. The back story? . . . All you need to know is that Yossele, with Hashem's help, has saved the world once already! He's not interested in being a hero, but only Hashem truly knows from whom salvation must come.

This gripping story will help us remember and internalize the idea that true heroism lies not in physical might, but in the spirit — man's spirit of self-sacrifice and his dedication to following in the path of Hashem. Each one of us has the power to change the world if only we choose good at every turn.

Planet Earth glows above the lunar skies, lending a bit of color to the bleak, monotonous landscape. The moon is desolate. There is no life here, not even plant life — just basalts, anorthosites, breccias, and dust. This area of the moon is strewn with broken pieces of an exploded American space station. Complete silence reigns.

But...a faint noise is heard from amidst the rubble. A slight scratching sound, some movement... *what could it be?*

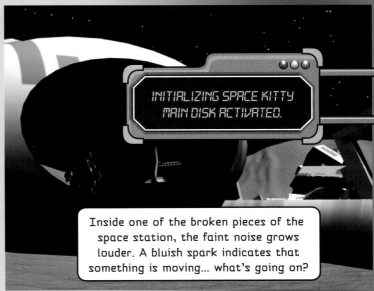

INITIALIZING SPACE KITTY MAIN DISK ACTIVATED.

Inside one of the broken pieces of the space station, the faint noise grows louder. A bluish spark indicates that something is moving... what's going on?

BEWARE! INTENSE RADIATION!

Yes, it's Kitty the robot. He's survived the explosion from our last adventure!

Unlike human beings, robots can survive the impact of a great fall. And they don't require oxygen, either. Kitty's strong yet flexible titanium alloy helped him survive the explosion. After he fell, Kitty managed to rise, crawl to a nearby opening, and survey the landscape. Now his sensors are warning him of radiation in the area! He picks his way out of the rubble and seeks an energy source where he can recharge himself.

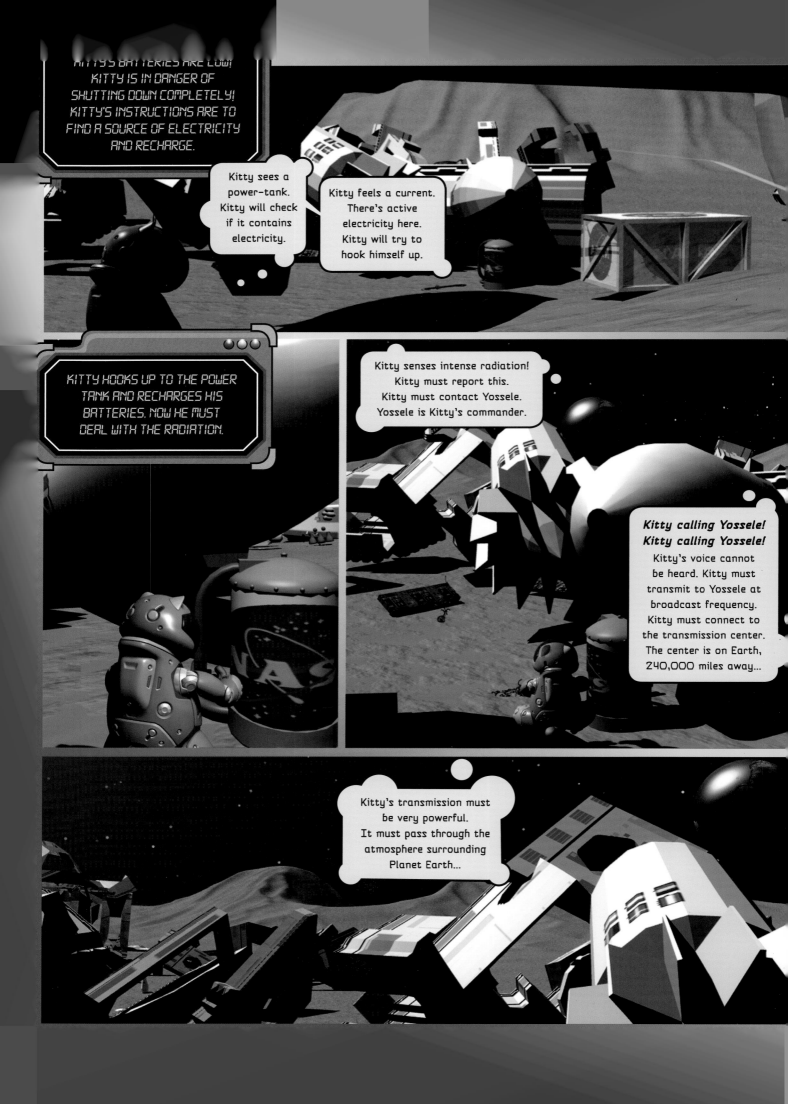

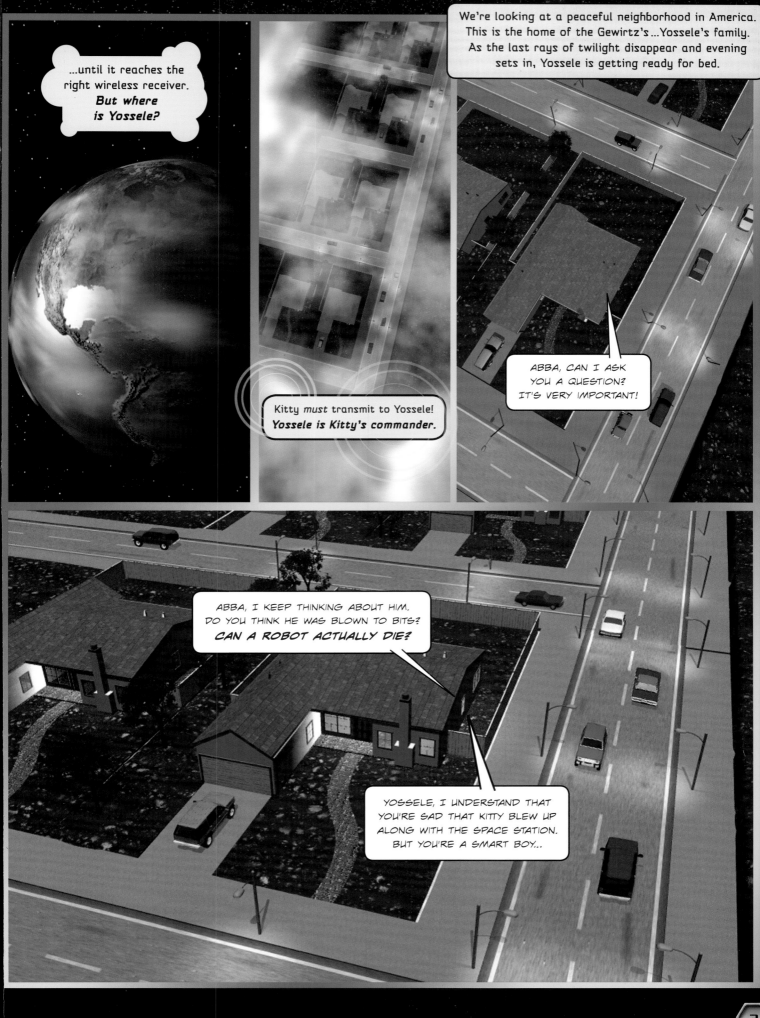

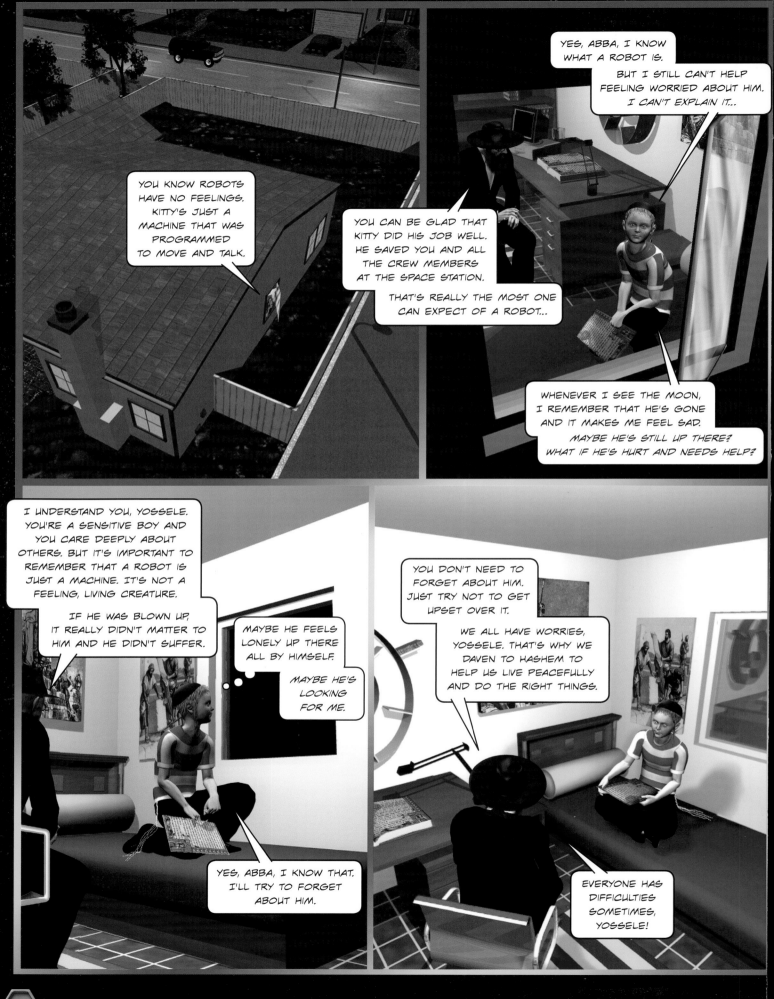

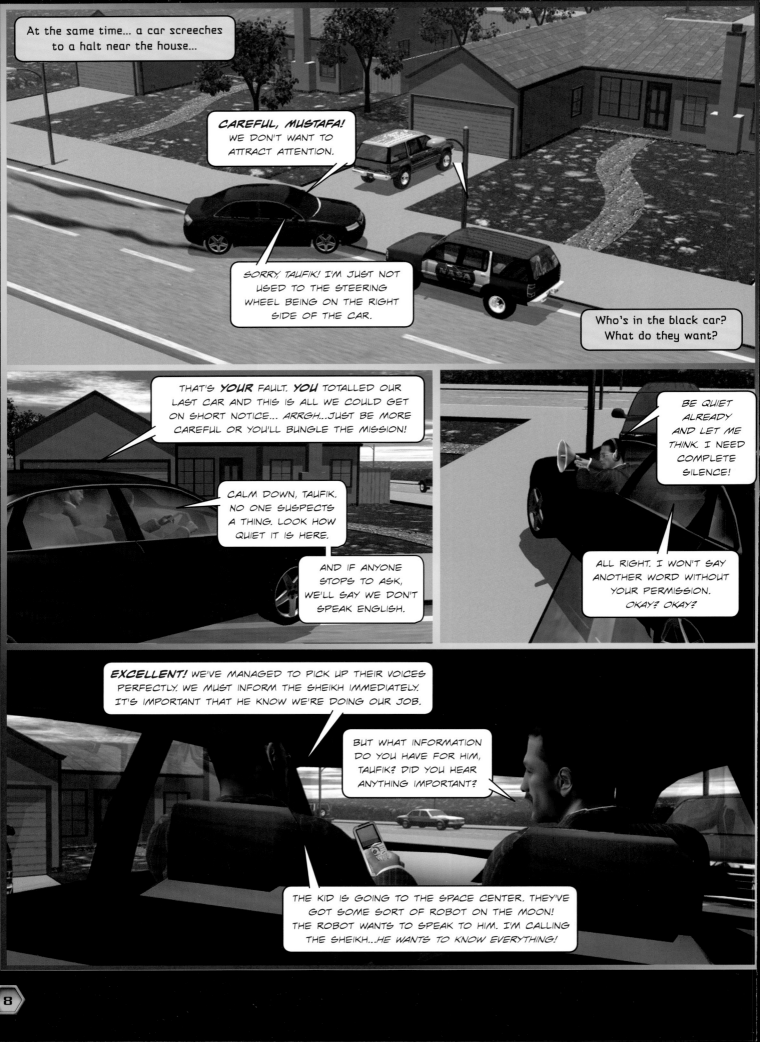

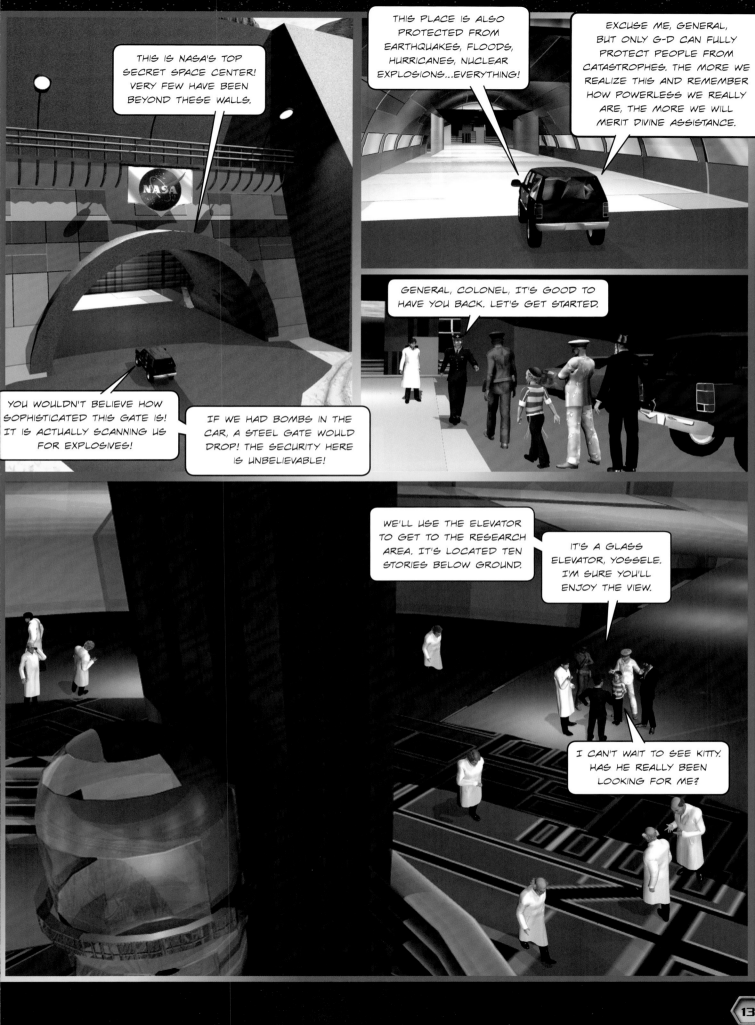

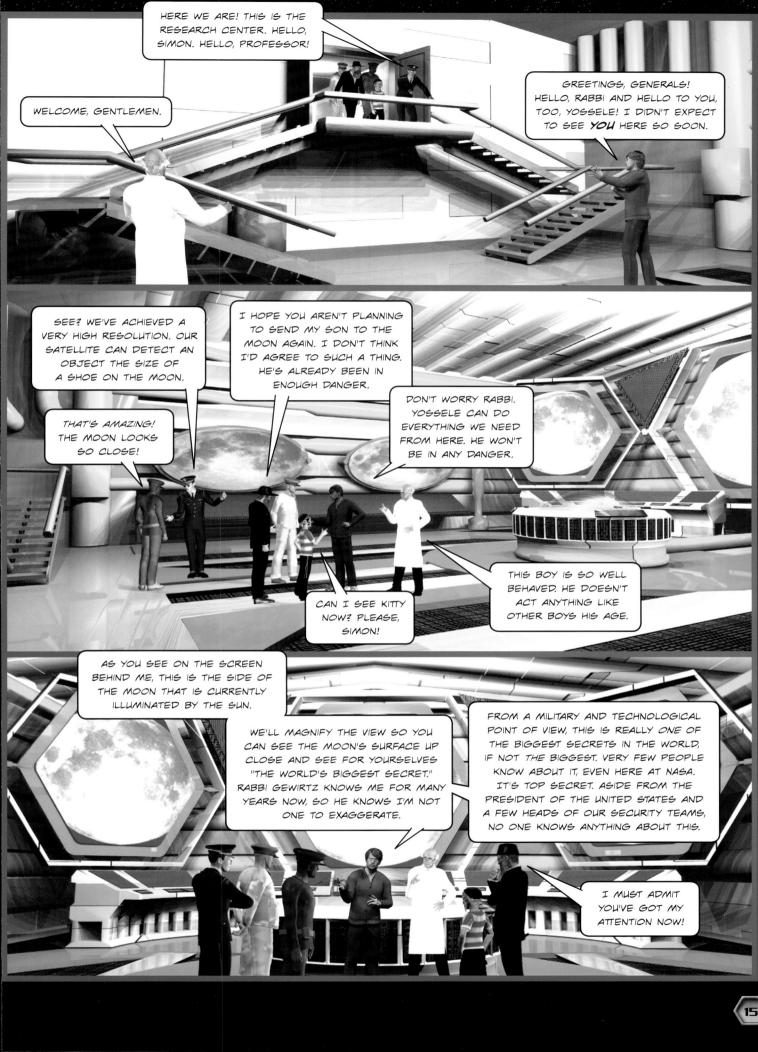

In the moon's weak gravity the astronauts remove the heavy equipment with ease.

OVER THE COURSE OF APOLLO'S REPEATED MISSIONS, ASTRONAUTS BUILT AN ENTIRE MILITARY BASE. THIS IS THE MOST SECRET MILITARY BASE IN THE WORLD. ITS GOAL IS TO MAKE SURE THAT NO ONE BESIDES THE U.S. CAN GET TO THE MOON.

THE ENTIRE BASE WAS BUILT WITH THIN, BUT STRONG, STEEL NETTING. IF NECESSARY, IT COULD BE OPENED AND MISSILES LAUNCHED. BILLIONS OF DOLLARS WERE INVESTED IN THE PROJECT.

AT THE TIME, RUSSIA AND AMERICA WERE ENGAGED IN A COLD WAR. TENSION BETWEEN THE TWO COUNTRIES RAN HIGH. AMERICA WORRIED ABOUT A POSSIBLE NUCLEAR ATTACK, SO THE BASE WAS EQUIPPED WITH THE MEANS TO LAUNCH MISSILES FROM THE MOON. NO OTHER COUNTRY HAD SUCH MILITARY SUPREMACY.

THIS IS HOW THE BASE LOOKED TOWARD THE END OF THE PROJECT—AN IMPRESSIVE STRUCTURE THAT WOULD ENSURE THE SECURITY OF THE UNITED STATES!

BUT THIS STRUCTURE, OF COURSE, WAS NOT MEANT TO BE SEEN. IMMEDIATELY AFTER ITS COMPLETION, THE ASTRONAUTS COVERED IT WITH A LAYER OF MOON DUST.

THE DUST COVERED THE ENTIRE STRUCTURE TO KEEP IT HIDDEN FROM THE LENS OF ANY TELESCOPE. THAT'S HOW THE HISTORIC MILITARY PLAN WAS COMPLETED: AN AMERICAN NUCLEAR MISSILE BASE—ON THE MOON!

BUT WE HAVEN'T YET REACHED THE MAIN PART OF THE STORY. HERE'S WHERE IT REALLY BEGINS!

WHAT A STORY!

AT THIS POINT, THE APOLLO PROJECT WAS OVER, AND THAT'S THE REASON PEOPLE DID NOT RETURN TO THE MOO

That evening: Rabbi Gewirtz and Yossele finally return home...

HAVE A SAFE TRIP HOME! GOOD NIGHT!

THANKS! WE'LL BE IN TOUCH TOMORROW.

I HOPE WE'LL FIND A SOLUTION AND YOSSELE WILL BE ABLE TO HELP US. TOMORROW WE'LL GATHER ALL OUR EXPERTS FOR A MEETING.

I ALSO HOPE WE'LL FINISH WITH THIS QUICKLY.

GOOD NIGHT! REGARDS TO KITTY!

COME IN YOSSELE. YOU LOOK EXHAUSTED. WOULD YOU LIKE A COLD DRINK?

NO THANKS, ABBA. I'LL BRING YOU A DRINK! I WANT TO DO THE MITZVAH OF KIBBUD AV. BESIDES, I'M NOT SO TIRED.

YOU'RE A REAL TZADDIK, YOSSELE. YOU ALWAYS THINK OF OTHERS BEFORE YOURSELF. I'M PROUD OF YOU.

WHAT CAN I SAY ABBA! I HAVE THE BEST TEACHER EVER...YOU!

A car moves along the road and stops quietly near the house.

YOSSELE, YOU MADE ME SO PROUD TODAY. G-D-WILLING THIS TEST WILL SOON BE BEHIND US!

I HOPE SO, TOO. GOOD NIGHT, ABBA.

What's going to happen next? What kind of visitors show up at such a late hour?

24

The fuel tanker departs and there is no trace of what happened...

BON VOYAGE!. ENJOY YOUR TRIP.

YOSSELE, LET'S SAY TEFILLAS HADERECH TOGETHER. ONLY HASHEM CAN HELP US NOW.

In the morning, two police cars with flashing lights and sirens pull up to the family's house.

THEY DIDN'T ANSWER MY CALLS, SO I BECAME SUSPICIOUS! I SENT THE POLICE OVER AND THEY DISCOVERED THAT THE FATHER AND SON WERE MISSING!

BUT THERE WERE NO SIGNS OF A STRUGGLE! DO YOU THINK THEY RAN AWAY? MAYBE THEY GOT FED UP WITH WORKING FOR NASA.

I'VE KNOWN THE RABBI FOR MANY YEARS. HE DOES WHAT HE THINKS IS RIGHT AND NEVER HESITATES TO VOICE HIS OPINION. HE WOULDN'T JUST RUN.

THE ONLY POSSIBLE EXPLANATION IS THAT THEY WERE ABDUCTED. BUT BY WHOM?

PREPARE THE STAFF. I'M COMING OVER. WE'LL PROBABLY HAVE TO BRIEF THE F.B.I. ON THE MATTER. NATIONAL SECURITY IS AT STAKE! IF SOMEONE ABDUCTED THEM, MAYBE HE WANTS TO USE THEM TO SEIZE CONTROL OF THE LUNAR BASE! BUT WE'LL HAVE TO KEEP THIS CONFIDENTIAL.

I'LL BRIEF EVERYONE. WE'LL PUT OUR HEADS TOGETHER AND TRY TO COME UP WITH SOMETHING.

THROW THEM IN A CELL AND GIVE THEM JUST BREAD AND WATER UNTIL THEY AGREE TO MY DEMANDS.

MR. FADALLAH, SHOW SOME COMPASSION. YOU KNOW WE CAN NEVER AGREE TO WHAT YOU'RE ASKING.

WE SHALL SEE. I'VE DEFEATED TOUGHER MEN THAN YOU.

IF YOU WANT TO SUFFER ON ACCOUNT OF THE AMERICANS THEN BE MY GUEST... IN PRISON! **OR** GET LOTS OF MONEY... YOUR CHOICE!

RABBI, TAKE THE OFFER! NO ONE WILL BE ABLE TO TRACE THE SOURCE OF THE MONEY. WE'LL MAKE IT LOOK LIKE YOU WON THE LOTTERY.

YOSSELE, MY BRAVE BOY. IF THEY THREATEN YOU THAT UNLESS YOU TRANSFER COMMAND OF KITTY TO THEM, THEY'LL KILL ME, IGNORE THEM. I DON'T WANT TO LIVE AT THE EXPENSE OF THOUSANDS OF VICTIMS.

IF YOU GIVE THEM KITTY, THEY'LL USE HIM TO SEIZE CONTROL OF THE MOON BASE AND THE NUCLEAR MISSILES. THEN ONE DAY THEY'LL SHOOT A MISSILE AT AMERICA OR ERETZ YISRAEL. PROMISE ME YOU WON'T DO IT, NO MATTER WHAT, YOSSELE.

IT PAINS ME TO HEAR YOU SAY THESE THINGS, ABBA. BUT I PROMISE I WON'T GIVE THEM KITTY. NOT EVEN IF THEY THREATEN TO KILL ME. BUT I BELIEVE THAT HASHEM WILL HELP US. DON'T WORRY, ABBA, WE'LL GET OUT OF HERE.

DEAR SHEIKH, YOU KNOW THE JEWS ARE A STIFF-NECKED PEOPLE. WHAT WILL WE DO IF THEY DON'T GIVE IN?

THEN I'LL HAVE TO MANAGE WITHOUT THEIR ROBOT! OUR CHINESE GUY IS COMPLETING AN EVEN BETTER SERIES OF ROBOTS FOR US NOW. WE'LL DISPATCH THEM QUICKLY, BEFORE THE AMERICANS PULL THEMSELVES TOGETHER OVER THERE.

DO WE HAVE ENOUGH NEW ONES, OR ARE YOU GOING TO TAKE FROM THE ROBOTS GUARDING HERE?

THE AMERICANS HAVE NO IDEA THAT WE'VE MANAGED TO DEVELOP SUCH HIGH-LEVEL ROBOTS. IF THEY FIND US, THEY'LL BE IN FOR A BIG SURPRISE! OUR ROBOTS WILL FINISH THEM OFF EASILY.

OUR CHINESE GUY WORKS DAY AND NIGHT! I MUST FIND A WAY TO MAKE HIM WORK EVEN **MORE**!

LET'S CALL HIM. HE WORKS ON THE LOWER LEVEL HERE.

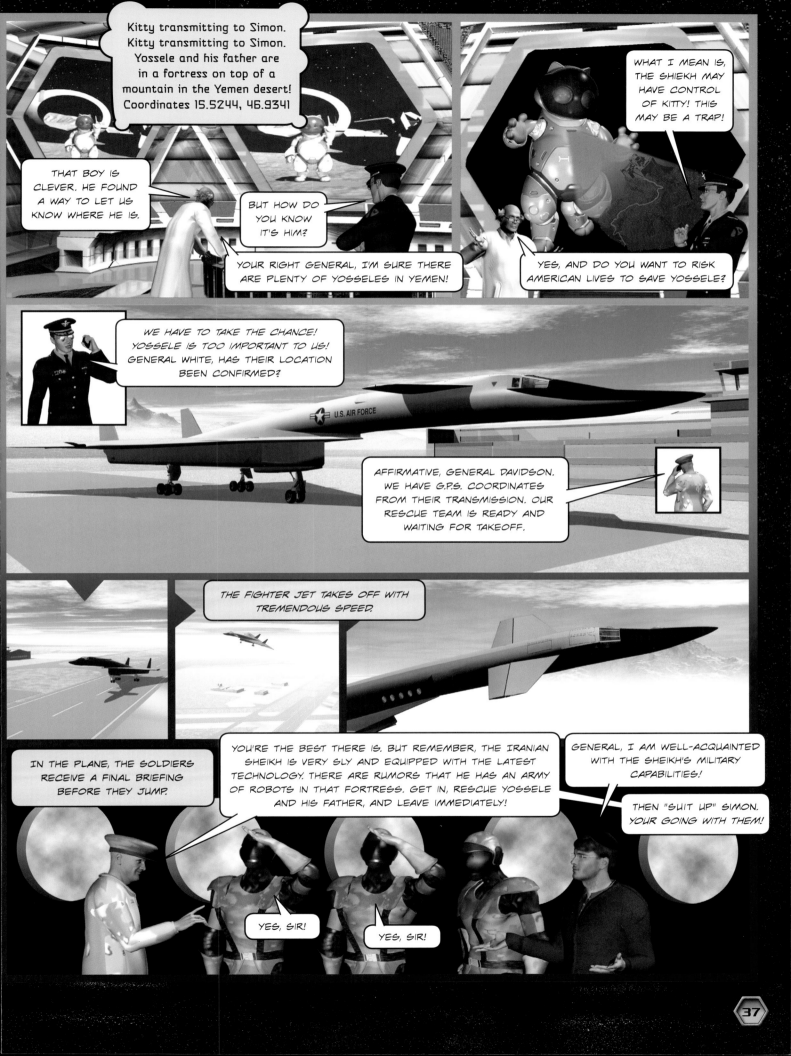

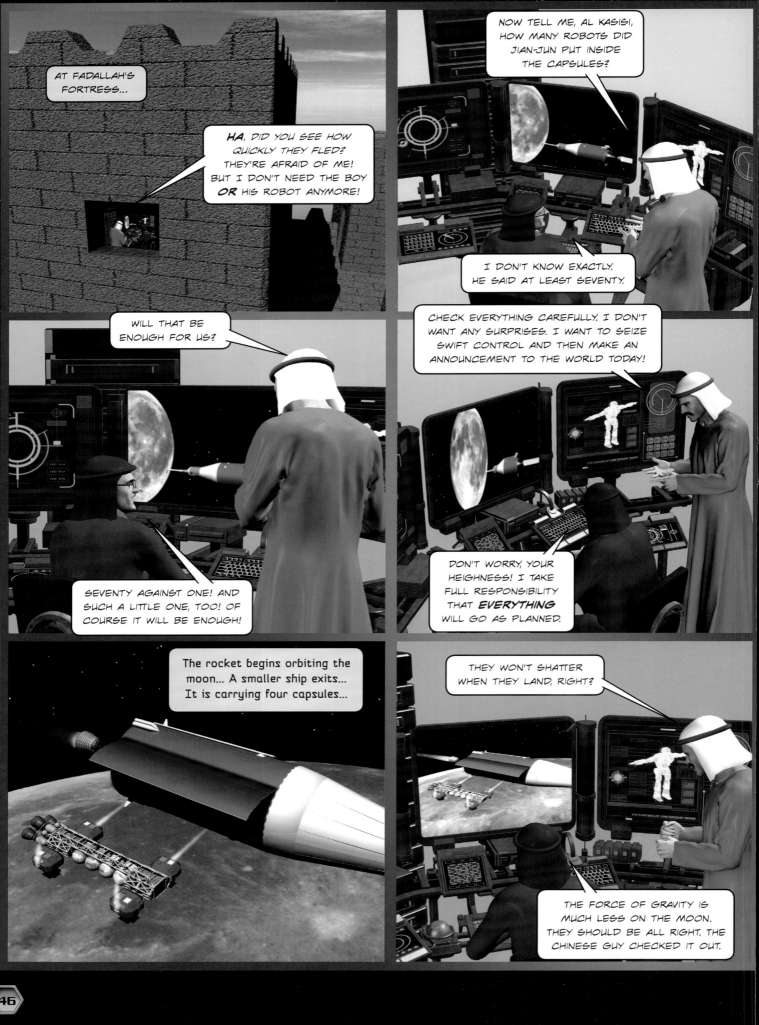

HEY, WHAT'S THAT?...THE SMALL ROBOT AND A HOLOGRAM OF THE JEWISH BOY. POWER-UP LASERS AND **ELIMINATE THEM!**

THE ROBOTS OPEN FIRE. NOTHING HAPPENS TO YOSSELE'S IMAGE, BUT KITTY IS IN DANGER...

At the last moment, Kitty manages to leap away and get out of the line of fire!

The robots turn and march to the gate of the lunar base.

IT'S INCREDIBLE! THEY'VE GOT VERY SOPHISTICATED ROBOTS!

I SUGGEST WE CUT THE POWER TO THE LUNAR BASE. THAT WAY THEY WON'T BE ABLE TO ACTIVATE THE CONTROL PANEL FOR THE MISSILES!

WITH ALL DUE RESPECT, PROFESSOR, THAT MIGHT MAKE IT EASIER FOR THEM TO GAIN CONTROL. ALL THE SECRET PASSWORDS WILL BE CANCELED.

MAYBE WE SHOULD SEND AN AMERICAN ROCKET UP. WOULD IT GET THERE IN TIME?

THAT WOULDN'T BE WISE. IT WOULD JUST GIVE THEM AN EXCUSE TO ATTACK AMERICA.

GENTLEMEN, I HAVE AN IDEA. IT WILL INVOLVE BOTH KITTY AND YOSSELE TOGETHER!

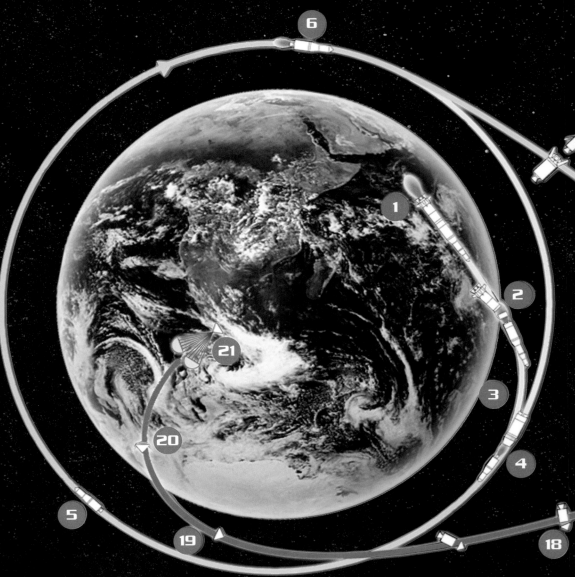

SATURN V
ROCKET

1. Saturn V lift-off
2. First stage separates and falls to the sea
3. Launch escape system is jettisoned
4. Second stage separates and falls to the sea
5. Achieving Earth "parking" orbit
6. Translunar injection
7. CSM separates, turns and docks with LM
8. 3rd stage separates and falls to Moon's surface
9. Midcourse correction
10. Achieving lunar orbit
11. LM/CSM separate
12. LM lands on Moon's surface
13. LM ascent stage lift-off
14. LM ascent stage/CSM rendezvous and docking
15. LM ascent stage jettisons and falls to Moon's surface
16. Trans-Earth injection
17. Mid-course correction
18. CM/SM separation
19. CM reenters into Earth's atmosphere
20. Communications blackout
21. Splashdown

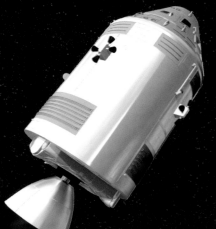

COMMAND &
SERVICE
MODULE (C.S.M.)

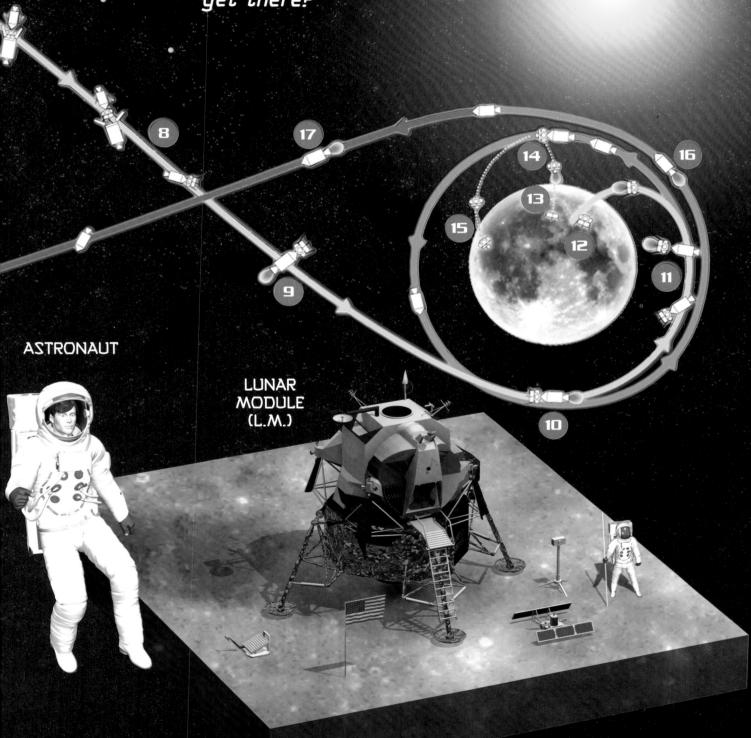

THE APOLLO MOON MISSIONS:

1961-1972

How did they get there?

ASTRONAUT

LUNAR MODULE (L.M.)

WHY IS THE MOON WHITE?

On 6 Av, 5729 (July 21, 1969), history was made when man first set foot on the moon. Two astronauts, Neil Armstrong and Edwin "Buzz" Aldrin, arrived there on the *Apollo 11*, an American spacecraft. The astronauts discovered that the moon was desolate, its surface made of basalts, anorthosites, and breccias, and covered with rock fragments and dust.

Hashem surrounded our Earth with a protective layer of atmosphere. When meteoroids from outer space fall through Earth's atmosphere, most of them burn up and disappear without causing any damage. Our moon, on the other hand, has no atmosphere and is constantly being bombarded by meteoroids both small and large, which pock its surface with craters of all sizes. This should serve as a constant reminder to us of what might have become of our planet, had Hashem not had mercy on us and provided us with an atmosphere. It gives us air to breathe, defends us from the sun's strong rays, and prevents large objects from outer space from reaching us.

Scientists today have incredibly powerful telescopes with which they spend hours examining billions of stars in numerous galaxies, but they have never found another planet with conditions as suitable for human sustenance as those we have on Earth. In fact, they have never found any other life forms except for those on our planet.

In the picture shown here, an astronaut is standing on the moon, with the beautiful, colorful Earth "shining" in the moon's skies.

A lack of atmosphere and plant life on the moon is the reason for its monotonous appearance, but that doesn't bother us. On the contrary, that's why the moon does a good job of illuminating our nights with a strong white light. In *lashon ha-kodesh*, the moon is referred to as the *levanah*, from the root word *lavan*, or white.

HOW THE SUN AND MOON AFFECT US

The two heavenly bodies that most affect our lives are, of course, the sun and the moon. The sun illuminates and warms Earth. It also illuminates the moon, which reflects this light back to us. (This idea is expressed in the holy Zohar [1:249]: "That is why the moon has no light of its own; rather, it gives light only when it is connected to the sun.")

Earth's gravitational force draws the moon toward it. And the moon, whose gravitational force is far less than planet Earth's, affects us in return. It causes the water in our oceans to rise upward, toward the moon, a phenomenon known as the rise and fall of the tide.

Due to the force of gravity, the moon always shows its same side to Earth. This side is called "the near side." The other side is always hidden from our eyes and is called "the far side." Sometimes, people refer to it as "the dark side," but that is inaccurate. As the moon orbits the earth, depending on its location, we are sometimes only able to see a portion of the illuminated side of the moon. This is why during the lunar cycle, our view of the moon's light changes over the course of a month. The beginning of each Hebrew month is marked by a tiny sliver of light from the moon. This is known as the *molad*.

The dark spots that can be seen on the moon are called *maria*, or seas, because early astronomers had assumed that these spots were bodies of water.

Another few facts and numbers: The moon is the celestial body closest to Earth. The average distance between the center of the moon and the center of Earth is approximately 238,857 miles. The moon's diameter is 2,159 miles, just a bit more than a quarter of Earth's diameter. The force of gravity on the moon is just one-sixth of that on Earth, which is why astronauts can carry very heavy loads while on the moon. The moon completes an orbit around Earth every 29.5 days (approximately). There is a huge disparity of temperatures on the moon. The illuminated "day" hours are exceedingly hot (212 degrees Fahrenheit) while the dark "night" hours can reach -274 degrees Fahrenheit!

Although flights to the moon have not yielded as many beneficial results to mankind as were hoped for (aside from technological advances that could have been procured via far cheaper means), space exploration is still a source of great prestige. Many countries, chiefly the US, continue their efforts – and spend billions of dollars – towards research that will enable manned space travel to the planets closest to Earth.

Approximately two years ago (5769), NASA made the dramatic announcement that water ice has been discovered in about 40 of the moon's craters in the north lunar pole, about 158 billion US gallons. However, this is not deemed enough of a reason to send astronauts back there anytime soon.

ECLIPSES:

LUNAR ECLIPSE

As explained above, the sun illuminates the moon and the moon reflects the sun's light back to Earth. When Earth moves exactly between the sun and the moon, it blocks the sun's light from reaching the moon, casting a "shadow" on it. As a result, we can see the moon slowly "darken" and fade from sight, either fully or partially. This phenomenon finishes when the moon continues its orbit and is no longer hidden by Earth. In this drawing, you can see the movement of the moon and the position in which a full lunar eclipse occurs.

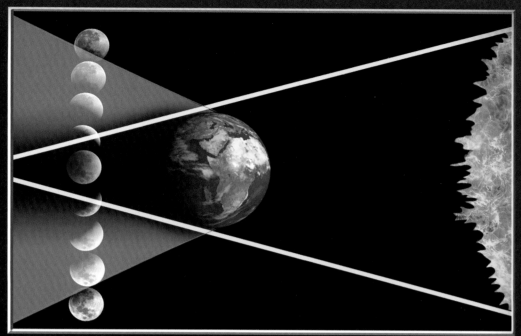

Lunar Eclipse: Earth casts a shadow on the moon

SOLAR ECLIPSE

A solar eclipse occurs when the moon lines up in its orbit between the sun and Earth, blocking Earth's view of the sun. Since the moon is smaller than the other two, it cannot cast a shadow on the entire Earth at once, but because it is much closer to Earth than the sun, it appears to be larger and the sun smaller. The moon then blocks our view of the sun or part of it from certain points on Earth. A full solar eclipse occurs when the moon is situated precisely opposite the sun. When this happens, it becomes dark in middle of the day, and only the halo surrounding the sun is visible.

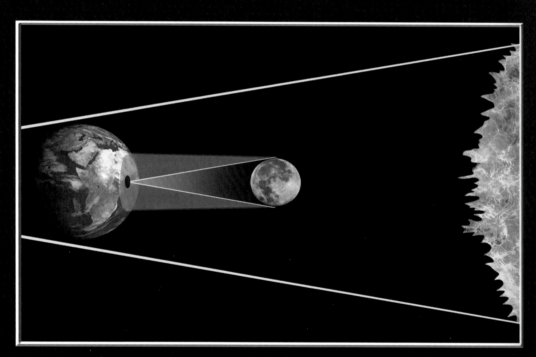

Solar Eclipse: The moon casts a shadow on our Earth.

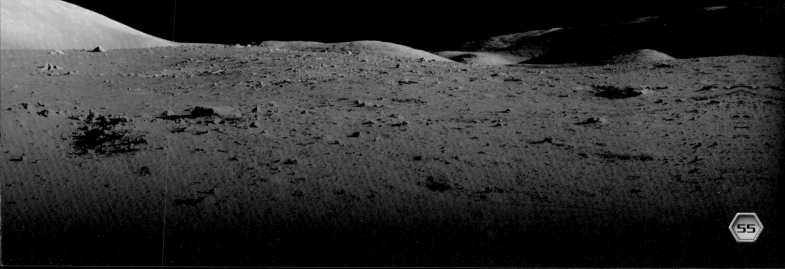